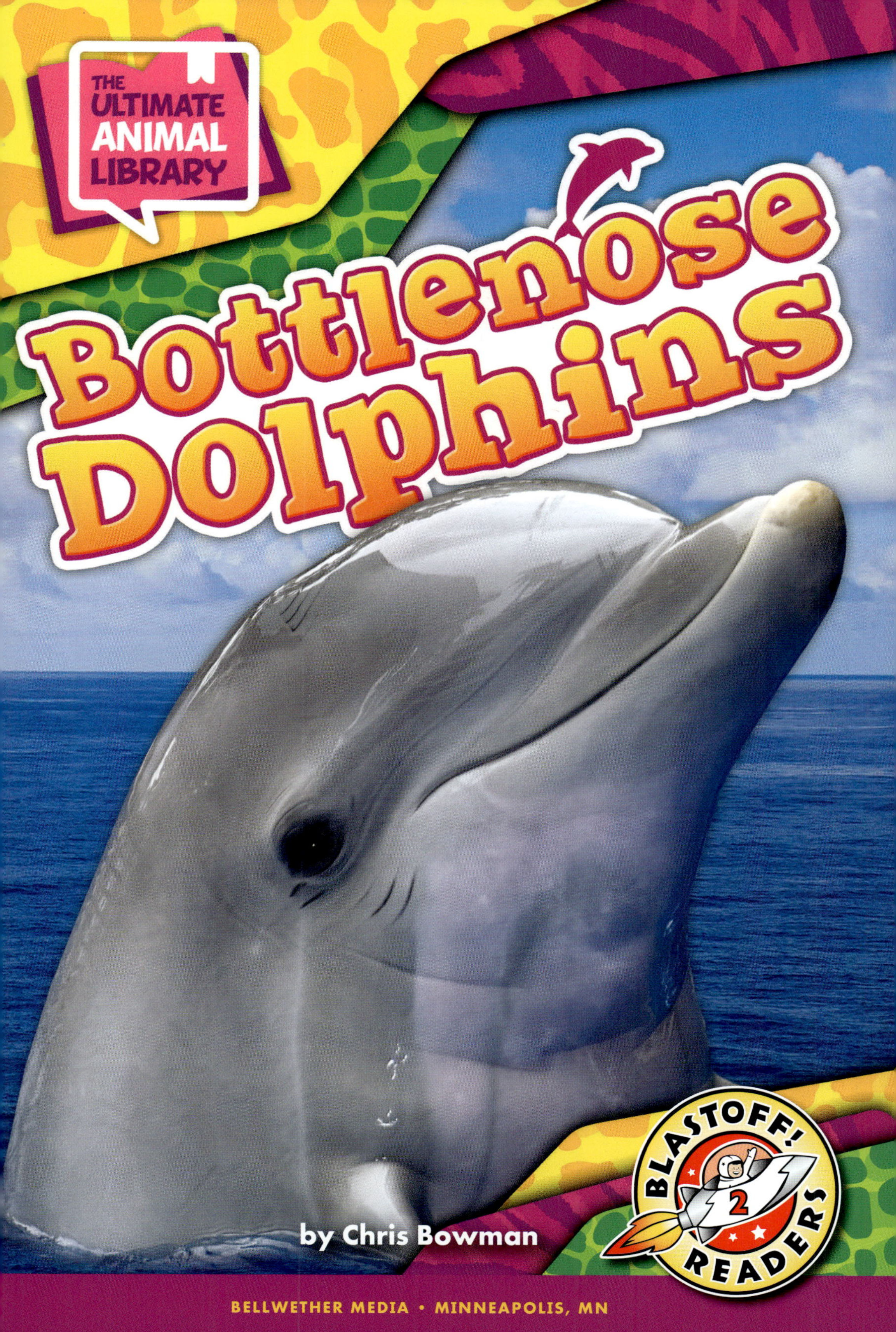
THE ULTIMATE ANIMAL LIBRARY
Bottlenose Dolphins
by Chris Bowman
BLASTOFF! 2 READERS
BELLWETHER MEDIA • MINNEAPOLIS, MN

Blastoff! Readers are carefully developed by literacy experts to build reading stamina and move students toward fluency by combining standards-based content with developmentally appropriate text.

LEVELS

Level 1 provides the most support through repetition of high-frequency words, light text, predictable sentence patterns, and strong visual support.

Level 2 offers early readers a bit more challenge through varied sentences, increased text load, and text-supportive special features.

Level 3 advances early-fluent readers toward fluency through increased text load, less reliance on photos, advancing concepts, longer sentences, and more complex special features.

★ **Blastoff! Universe**

Reading Level

Grade K

Grades 1–3

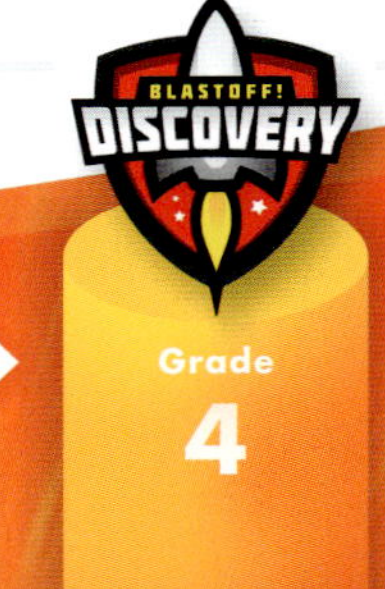

Grade 4

This edition first published in 2025 by Bellwether Media, Inc.

Library of Congress Cataloging-in-Publication Data

LC record for Bottlenose Dolphins available at: https://lccn.loc.gov/2024012115

Editor: Elizabeth Neuenfeldt Series Designer: Veah Demmin

Printed in the United States of America, North Mankato, MN.

Table of Contents

What Are Bottlenose Dolphins?

Bottlenose dolphins are ocean animals. They are named for their pointy **snouts**. These **mammals** can be big. Some grow up to 14 feet (4.3 meters) long!

Common Bottlenose Dolphin Report

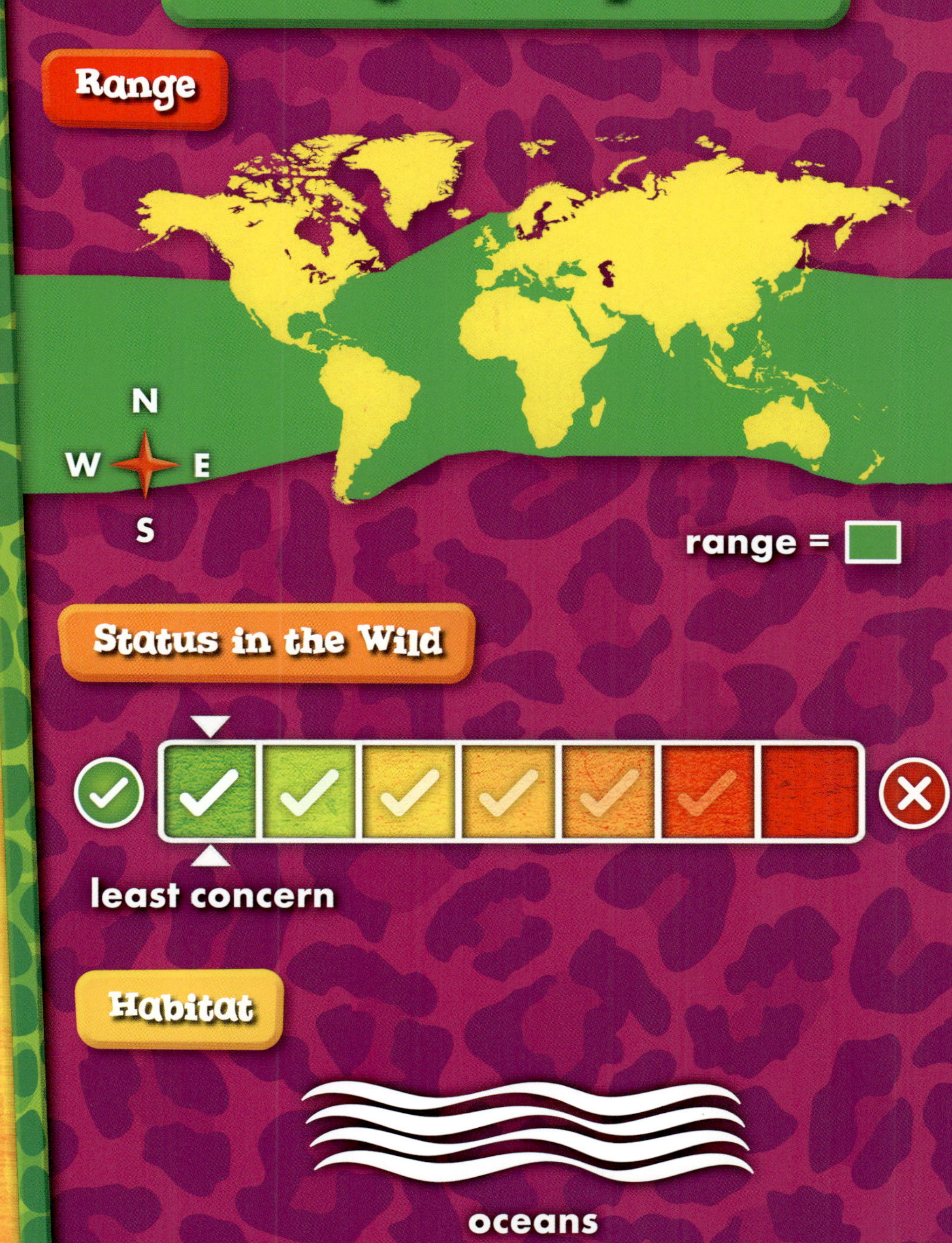

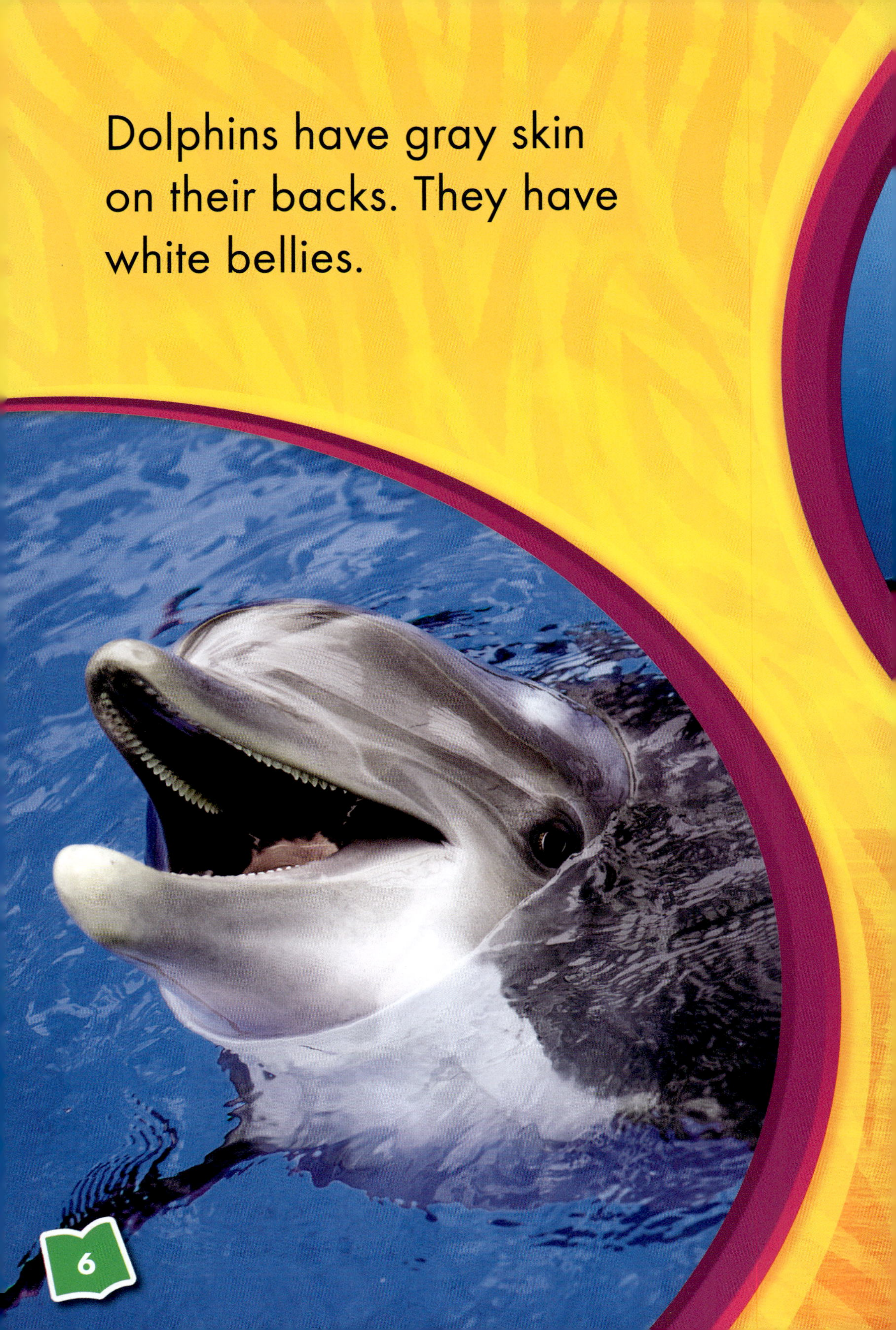

Dolphins have gray skin on their backs. They have white bellies.

They blend in with bright waters above them and dark waters below them.

fin

flippers

Bottlenose dolphins use their **flippers** to steer. Fins on their backs help them **balance**.

Their tails have two **flukes**.

Bottlenose dolphins breathe above the water. They breathe through **blowholes**. These are on top of their heads.

They hold their breath when they dive.

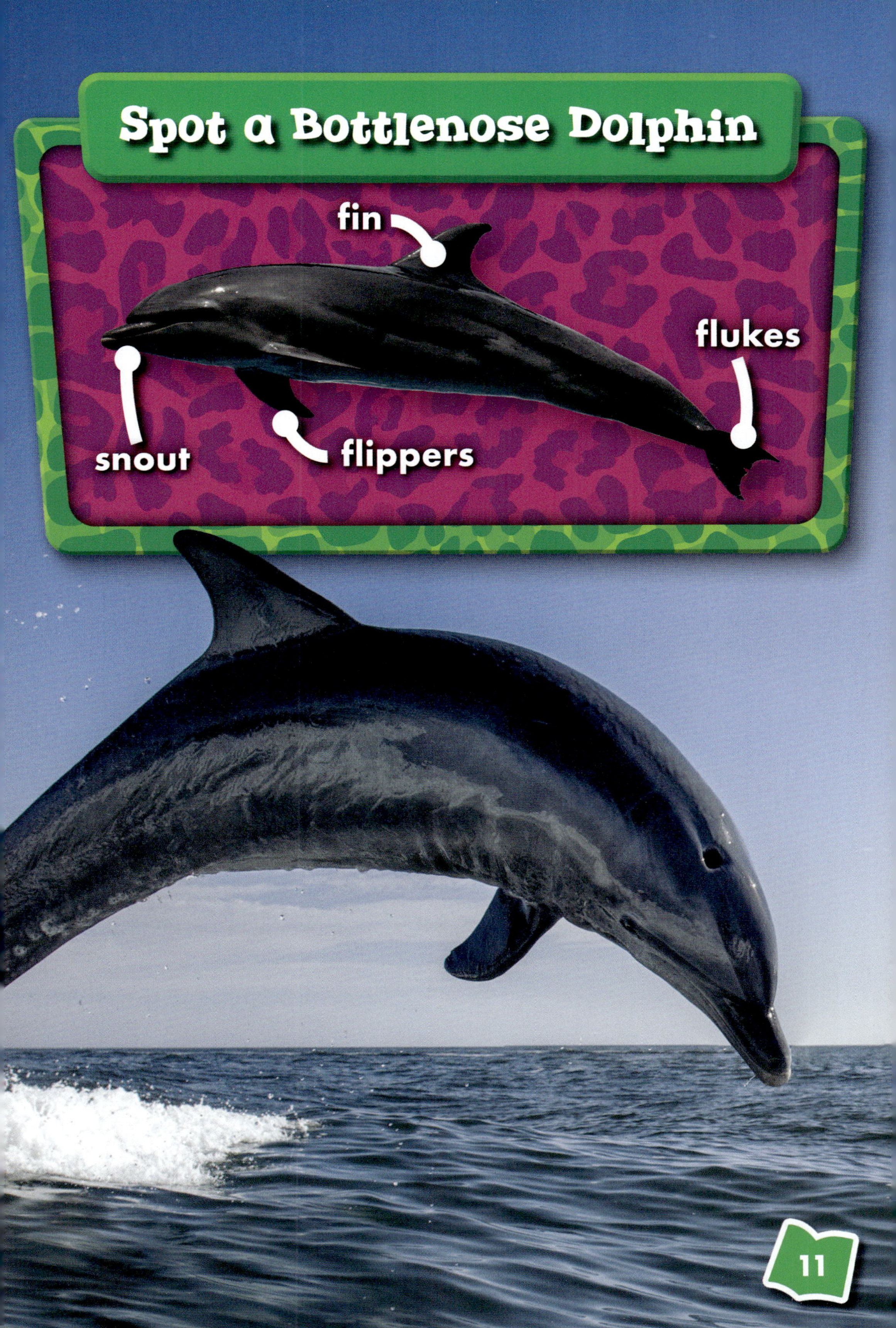
Spot a Bottlenose Dolphin
fin
flukes
snout
flippers

Social Swimmers

Bottlenose dolphins live in warm ocean waters around the world.

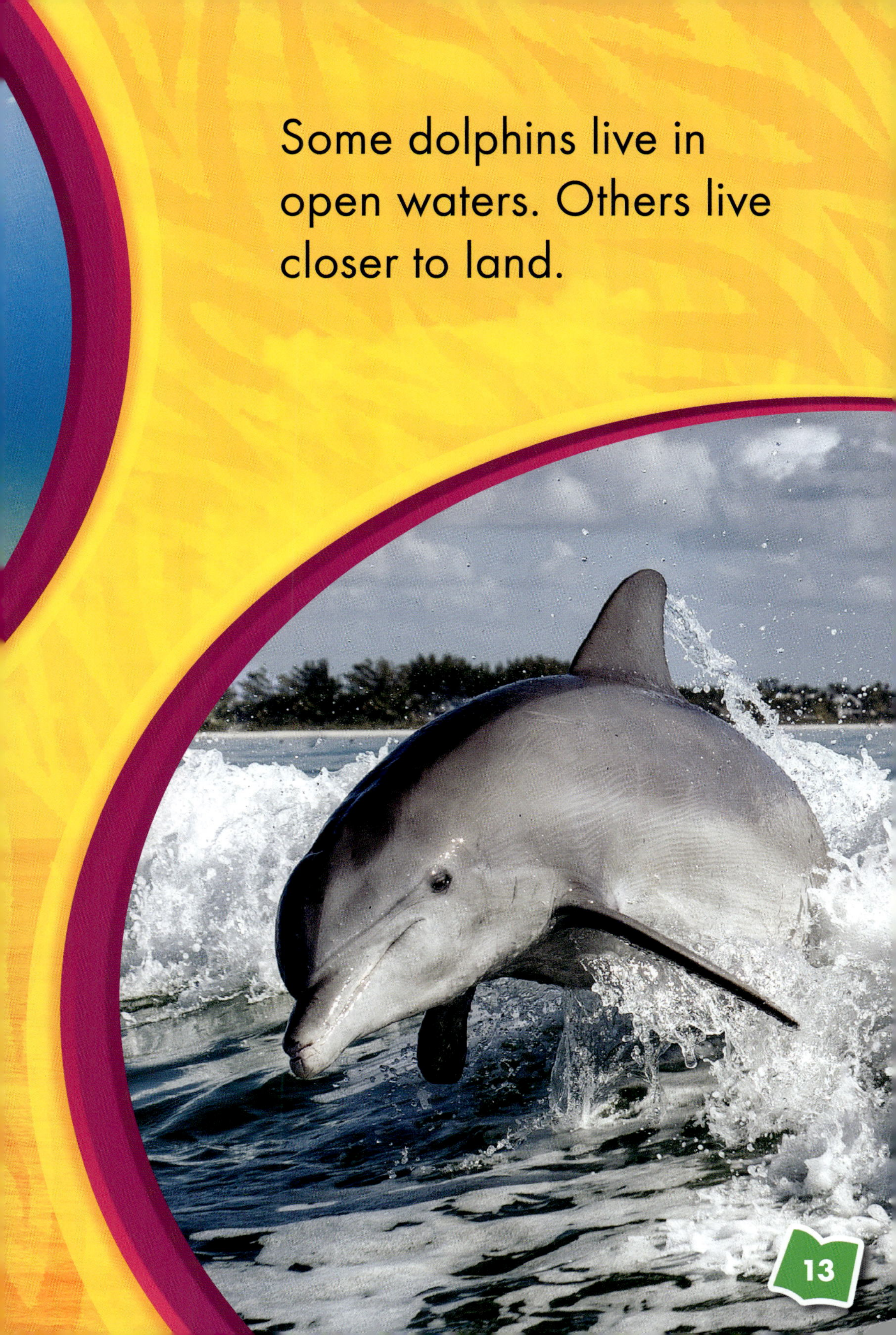

Some dolphins live in open waters. Others live closer to land.

Bottlenose dolphins are social animals. They click and squeak to talk to each other.

Many dolphins swim in **pods**. They stay safe from **predators** like sharks.

Bottlenose dolphins usually hunt alone. Sometimes pods work together to catch fish.

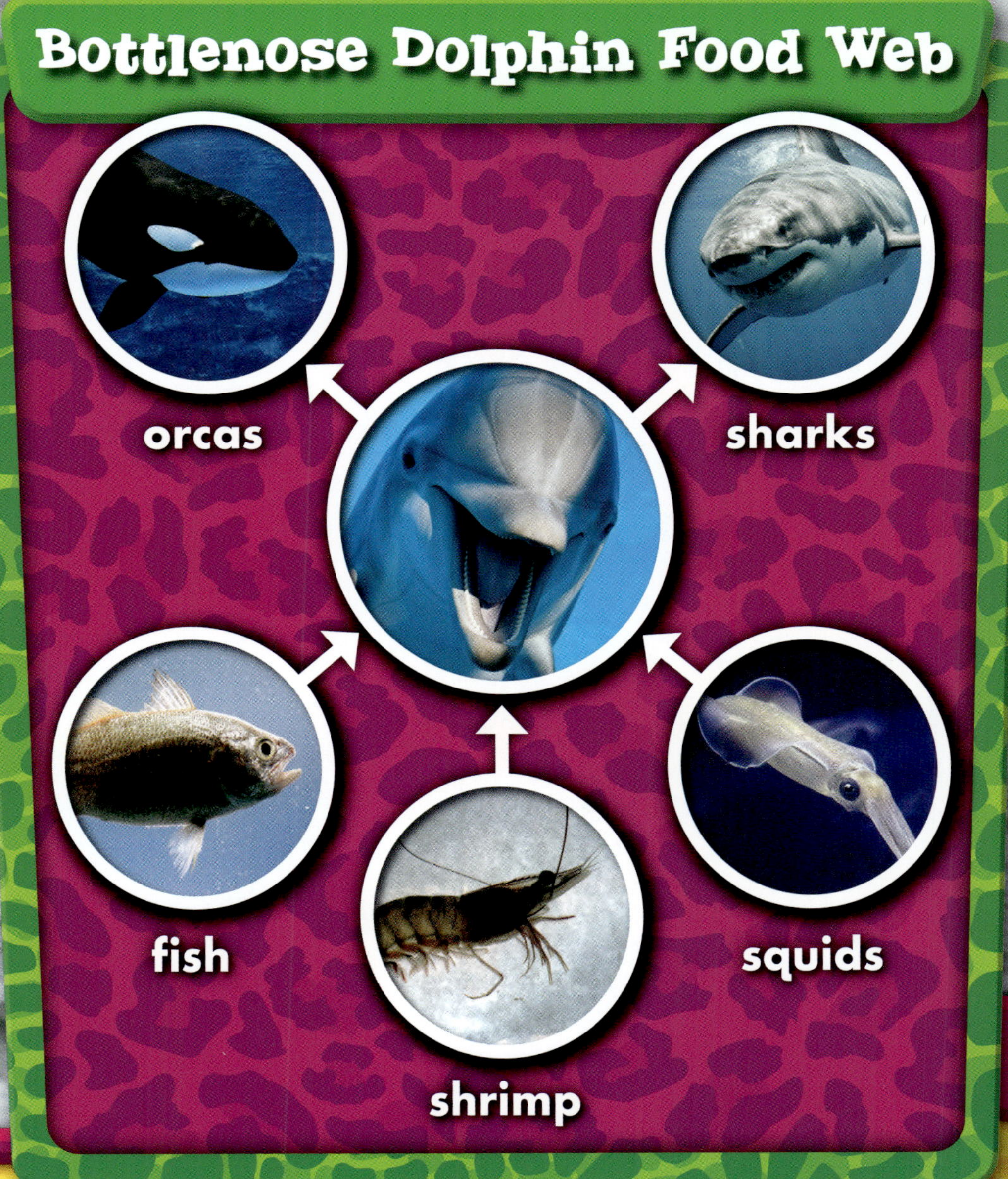

They also dive for shrimp and squids. They use **echolocation** to find **prey**.

Growing Up

Bottlenose dolphins give birth once every few years. They raise one **calf** at a time.

Calves drink milk from their mothers for one or two years.

calf

Calves stay with their
mothers for up to six years.
Calves learn to find food.

Then the newly grown-up dolphins find a new pod!

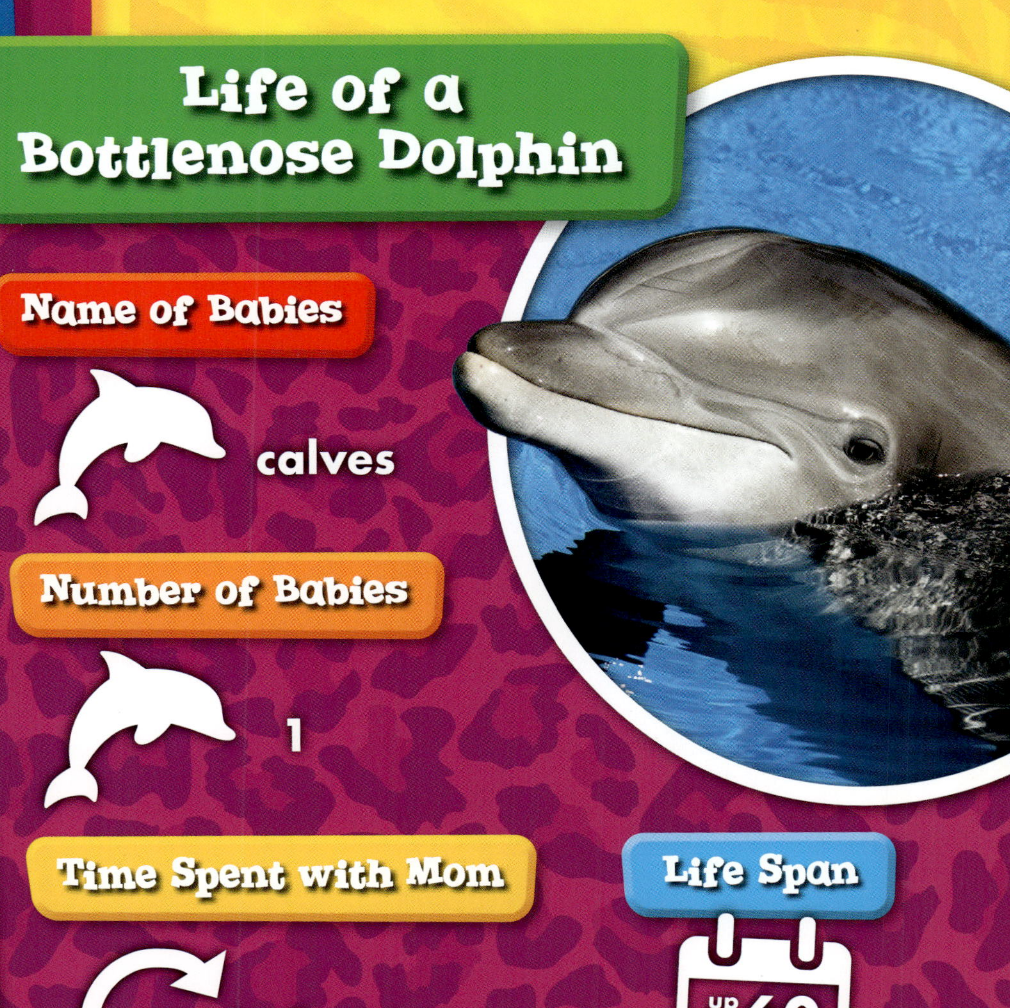

Glossary

balance–to stay upright

blowholes–holes on the top of dolphins' heads that are used for breathing

calf–a baby dolphin

echolocation–the process of finding objects or animals using sound waves

flippers–wide, flat body parts that are used for swimming

flukes–fins on dolphins' tails that are used for swimming

mammals–warm-blooded animals that have backbones and feed their young milk

pods–groups of dolphins

predators–animals that hunt other animals for food

prey–animals that are hunted by other animals for food

snouts–the noses and mouths of some animals

To Learn More

AT THE LIBRARY

Mattern, Joanne. *Dolphins.* Minneapolis, Minn.: Bellwether Media, 2021.

Scheffer, Janie. *Humpback Whales.* Minneapolis, Minn.: Bellwether Media, 2025.

Schuh, Mari. *Dolphins.* Minneapolis, Minn.: Jump!, 2022.

ON THE WEB

FACTSURFER

Factsurfer.com gives you a safe, fun way to find more information.

1. Go to www.factsurfer.com.
2. Enter "bottlenose dolphins" into the search box and click 🔍.
3. Select your book cover to see a list of related content.

Index

The images in this book are reproduced through the courtesy of: InnaPoka, series patterns; Izoe, cover background, interior background; Nicolas-SB, cover (bottlenose dolphin); ILYA AKINSHIN, cover (dolphin icon); New Africa, p. 3; Tory Kallman, pp. 4, 10-11, 13; Irina No, pp. 6, 21; gilkop, p. 7; Nigel Marsh, p. 8; Grafissimo, p. 9; Lady_Luck, p. 10; chonlasub woravichan, p. 11; Martin Strmiska/ Alamy, pp. 12, 14; Ramon Carretero, pp. 15, 17 (sharks); David Jefferson/ Alamy, pp. 16-17; slowmotiongli, p. 17 (orcas); twygg, p. 17 (dolphin); NOAA/NMFS/SEFSC Pascagoula Labratory/ Wikipedia, p. 17 (fish); NOAA's Estuarine Research Reserve Collection/ Wikipedia, p. 17 (shrimp); Lauren Squire, p. 17 (squids); Jerome Murray - CC/ Alamy, p. 18; NaluPhoto, pp. 18-19; Norbert Probst/ Getty, p. 20; Vince Scherer, p. 23.